The Time of Your Life

a simple guide - because your life is not a rehearsal

Tony Brady

ISBN: 9798722784544

DEDICATION

To my ever-encouraging wife Fran
who will be looking to see these ideas in action in the days ahead

The Time of Your Life

CONTENTS

ACKNOWLEDGMENTS

To Tom Evans who encouraged me to end the procrastination and launch these long-delayed ideas out into the world

The Time of Your Life

Part 1 – Why? – Who? – How?

A – Welcome, and why this book?

Why yet another book on Time Management? Well, why not? Can we ever say we have enough advice about the management of our time?

Every new day is an unearned gift of incredible value, and surely all of us would wish to make the best use of the time available to us.

Most of us are inclined, especially when we are young, to feel that we have an endless supply of days, that is, if we think of the matter at all. But of course, that idea of an infinite supply of days is not the reality we face. On some unknown date, which we all hope will be far into the future, our supply of time will run out. We see this happening to other people all the time, but we find it hard to accept that it will happen to us.

This thought is not to encourage a morbid over-preoccupation with our own demise. That would be a depressing way to fill the days which it is our good fortune to have. But we would all benefit by paying a little more attention to the reality of our time-limited existence here.

Most of us rarely stop to consider the discomforting fact that our lives will one day come to an end. Even when that reality crosses our minds, we imagine (and hope) the inevitable event is quite some time away.

As we age, we become more aware of the reality of our limited life expectancy as human beings. But we still have difficulty imagining that our particular enjoyment of, and contribution to, the general wellbeing of the world might end this year, this month, this week or even this very day.

So, as we awake to the light of each new day and as we give thanks for our life renewed each morning, can we learn to find ways to spend the hours of each new day as carefully as we spend the money we earn? After all, with additional effort and by working harder or more efficiently, most people can manage to bring in more money. With careful attention to our diet, exercise and lifestyle, we can work to improve our chances of a longer life. But unlike our supply of money, which can, for the most part, be added to indefinitely, there is a point in time where, despite all our best efforts and all the advances of medical science, we will have to bid farewell to this world.

The realisation that our life's time is limited calls for a response of some sort from each of us. Now I am not suggesting that you should fill every available minute with frenetic activity. But I imagine we would all like to see that we have spent a reasonable amount of our time in a way that allows us to look back on our lives with some degree of satisfaction. None of us will want to look back and see that the gift of our lives is something that we have neglected, taken for granted and allowed to pass heedlessly through our fingers.

I hope that by putting some of these ideas into practice, you will be better able to look back with fewer regrets in the years to come.

Enjoy the journey.

B – Who might benefit from this book?

This book is for a broad audience. I hope everyone will find it helpful in organising life at home. All of us are at home at some point, and I believe we will all benefit by putting some of these organisational ideas into effect in the place where we live.

Some readers will be employees who find themselves with helpers and other people under their charge. They will benefit by following this book's advice on delegation and assigning tasks and duties to people who can assist them with the completion of projects.

On the other hand, many employees will have no one to whom they can allocate part of the work. They have to do their job without the aid of an assistant. I believe they will find this book helpful in improving their own efficiency and effectiveness.

Self-employed people know they need to gather up all the helpful advice they can find. I hope they will find ideas here, which will help to make their lives easier. Self-employed people are in charge of their affairs. This fact means they can more easily change their practices straightway on receipt of every good idea.

CEOs with many people under their charge will find that many tips in this book can be put into effect as they improve efficiency, effectiveness and happiness throughout their organisations.

But there is more to life than its efficiency. We increase efficiency to gain time, not enable us to do even more work, however enjoyable that work may be. The aim is to gain time for living a more enjoyable and fulfilling life outside the paid job.

In this book, I hope you will find motivational suggestions and ideas that will allow you to look back and feel that, most of the time, you have made good use of the extraordinary gift that is the Time of Your Life.

C - How to get the most out of this book

I do not expect that you will read this book straight through from cover to cover, but I hope that, over time, you will read it all and that you will apply many of its suggestions. The book is intended to be read a chapter at a time but not in any particular order. When you find a good idea, make sure to take a little trouble to apply the concept in the week in which you read it.

I would suggest you look at the chapter titles appearing in the index, locate something on which you think you might need some help, then read that chapter for a start. Try to apply something from that chapter to your life this very week. Next week, look up another topic and consider doing the same.

We all enjoy sixty minutes of every hour and twenty-four hours of every day. Yet some people, more than others, manage to get a lot more done in that same time. Indeed, some people are happier than others when they consider how they have applied themselves. This book will help you to join that content group.

This book is not an appeal to fill every unforgiving minute with sixty second's work of distance run. Already many of our lives are more than filled with deadlines and multiple conflicting objectives. We endure pretty much enough of this treadmill of activity. Instead, this book aims to reduce the amount of time you will spend on the treadmill. I hope it will free some of your time for people and projects that matter to you.

Here you will find a collection of suggestions as to how you can more efficiently use the Time of Your Life. There are many things you have planned to do "someday". You persuade yourself that you will get around to these plans "when you have the time". But ask yourself, "When will I have any more time than I have now?". Time passes, and you can find ideas that are still lingering in the back of your mind. My long-delayed production of the book is a very case in point, and this book itself was a someday plan that was too long postponed. Years can slip by before we realise it, and sometimes we find the hopes and dreams of a lifetime are still sitting on the back burner at the end. This loss of time is something that I hope will be less likely to happen to you if you invest a little time, week by week, to follow the suggestions contained in this book.

At the end of each chapter, you will see a summary of the points that have been covered in that chapter. Use these as quick reminders of what you have read and a quick and easy refresher for you whenever you glance back through this book.

As you read, remember to take note of particular points that apply to your specific situation. Make sure too that you take notice of any good resolutions once you have made them. It is better to find one good idea and decide to apply it rather than run through the book, chapter after chapter, without taking note of something that will improve your time management. Each chapter should trigger a response from you in the form of a beneficial practice.

The good news is that this book does not require that you sit down and work out your life goals before proceeding to take your first step. The simple idea is to gain a little time here, a little time there, increase efficiency just a fraction here, a fraction there, avoid duplication of effort, and make use of snippets of time that might otherwise be lost.

With that extra time, you will be rewarded with a greater sense of direction and satisfaction in your life. You will gain the opportunity and the ability to plan for a future more of your own making.

Keep this book in a place where you will have the temptation to pick it up and fish for an idea whenever you find you have a few minutes to spare.

Summary of this chapter:

- This book is intended as an easy read. Pick a chapter, find an idea, take a note.

- Give the idea a chance to become a habit, and the benefits will speak for themselves.

- Look at the chapter names and see where you can begin to save some of the Time of Your Life. You are living the Time of YOUR Life, to be applied as YOU decide. I wish you every success in this endeavour.

Tony Brady – Dublin – March 2021

Part 2 - Getting Things Done

"I have been impressed with the urgency of doing. Knowing is not enough; we must apply. Being willing is not enough; we must do."

– Leonardo da Vinci

Chapter 1 - Why me? Why anyone?

Most of us have a natural tendency to wish to please. We have this basic impulse to say "yes" when our help is requested. Perhaps this arises from a deep-seated wish to be liked, a fear of being rejected. We desire not to offend someone who proposes something, even if it is a proposal that involves a substantial commitment of our time. You must curb this natural weakness if you wish to maintain some control of your time.

When any new proposition arises, the first question you must ask yourself is this: "Is this task something which ought to be done at all by anyone?" If the answer is still "yes", then and only then does the second question arise, "Can or should this be done by me?"

So how can you overcome this tendency to immediately say "yes" when you would prefer to say "no"? It is not easy, but you must begin somewhere. In the early stages of your transformation, a simple solution might be the following; you will think about the proposal with a promise to come back to the proposer with your answer a little later on. This response gives you a chance to consider the suggestion rationally, and it allows you time to consider your response taking into account your existing commitments. Then in the quietness of your own space, you can examine what is involved and decide whether the project is something you can and should undertake.

If your considered answer is "yes", then you can take up the task with the enthusiasm which comes from having decided in its favour. You will not be troubled by the nagging feeling that perhaps if you have made time to consider the matter, you should have said "no".

If, on the other hand, your decision is "no", then you will have granted the proposer the respect of having given careful consideration to the project. Your answer arises from a complete and logical review of whether the proposition can be comfortably added to your existing commitments. You will also experience the relief of not having been unthinkingly committed to something outside your current capacity.

But the awkward question remains, how do you manage to convey your "no" without offending? Your response is best kept simple. You are pleased to have been asked, you have considered the project and what it involves, you are sorry, but the answer must be "no". There should be no need to explain your list of existing commitments that give rise to your decision. Taking on a project is a matter for yourself, and you should not have to stand trial over it. Reciting your long list of other commitments will only prove counterproductive. It will add needlessly to any feelings of disappointment, or even resentment and anger, on the proposer's part. By reciting all you have on your hands, you will be demonstrating that this project has not been taken on board while at the same time listing all else that you so freely admit to being able to manage. Responding with excuses like that is never a good idea.

From time to time, stand back and examine your existing commitments in light of the limited number of hours in the day and the limitless number of potential calls on your time. Only you can take charge of the time of your life and decide rationally what you can do and what you wish to do and distinguish this from what you cannot or do not want to do. Sometimes we continue to do something only because we started, and we find ourselves unable to stop because of the fear of offending someone, especially if that someone is well known to us.

By re-examining your commitments objectively from time to time, you will free up time for the work and duties that you believe represent the most worthwhile expenditure of your time. In suggesting that you should not be someone who always says "yes", I am not encouraging you to become a member of the group of people who always say "no". What a pity that would be. What you decide to undertake does not have to be paid work or work that produces any reward other than the satisfaction attached to its own doing. In an increasingly busy society, there is a greater need for people who will give their time freely to voluntary work and community effort. Target your time on projects that mean a lot to you and make your contribution there with the enthusiasm that comes from being an authentic volunteer.

Summary of this chapter:

- Don't automatically say "yes" when you are asked to take on something new but don't fall into the habit of automatically saying "no."

- Take time to decide and carefully consider the new request in light of your existing commitments.

- Don't explain at length if your answer is "no". But if your answer is "yes", take on the project with the enthusiasm and energy of an authentic volunteer.

Chapter 2 - Do, Dump, Delegate or Delay

Just consider the number of letters, memos, papers, notes and emails that you come across in a day, in a week, in a year. You may have come across a piece of organisational wisdom that encourages you to handle a piece of paper or information as little as possible and, if at all possible, only once. That is a wise piece of advice.

An illustration:

Something lands in front of you. You take it up, read it, and you think a little about it. You decide you need to reflect a little more about it, and you put it to one side "just for now". It sits "for attention soon". But in a little while, it is joined by others. They, too, sit there innocently, all examined once, but none actioned. All remain "for attention".

Consider the time saving if you could train yourself this week to observe the rule that we have referred to above. Handle things as little as possible, and, if at all possible, only once.

An example:

Something comes in; you have resolved to do/dump/delegate or deliberately delay. The incoming item is useless. It goes straight to the bin without a second thought or any ambiguous feeling of "maybe". You have handled it only once. No agonising. Well done.

The next item is a matter that concerns someone else. You pass it on to the person concerned. It, too, has been handled only once. Good.

Your next step will be to sort matters which need your own attention into categories according to priority and urgency. (See Chapter 20 - Action Sorter) It is essential that these matters for attention not be left in a single unsorted lot but in groups or folders that will put them in a place where they can be found and given the required attention at the appropriate time. The holding areas will likely be in folders on your computer. If the items in question are physical items, you should place them in separate physical storage areas, trays, baskets, etc.

Items of lesser importance but still needing attention at some point should be kept in a place of their own and recalled for attention at certain pre-decided times. You can tackle this group earlier if an unexpected few minutes present themselves. But it is crucial to allocate a definite time, at least one a month, for these items of lesser importance. Otherwise, they can themselves accumulate out of control. If these matters need attention at all, you need to attend to them in an organised way.

So, avoid temporising. Develop the habit of automatically putting incoming items into their respective categories when you first look at them. Remember, this advice does not mean you should spend your day monitoring your inbox and allowing it to rule you. Remember too that papers and emails seem to exert a gravitational force all of their own. If you leave them to themselves, you will find that incoming documents and emails seem to gather around themselves a planet-like assortment of orbiting satellites. If you don't believe this, look at that state of all those uncared-for inboxes or confused desktops.

Sorting out, as suggested in this chapter, should not be left to chance. Otherwise, you will find yourself searching and rummaging through an over piled-up inbox or in-tray like a dog in search of a lost bone.

Some people have a fear of moving items from their physical desk or their computer desktop. This fear arises because they have failed to establish a working system for dealing with priorities. Rightly (in their case), these people believe that "out of sight" will mean "out of mind". We all need to do, dump, delegate or deliberately delay. To do this successfully, you must establish your priorities. Then you can maintain a clear desk, a clear desktop and a manageable inbox, and you need not be afraid that you will overlook anything of importance.

Summary of this chapter:

- Avoid temporising. Try to handle items only once, do it now, dump it now, delegate it now, or delay. A decision to delay or postpone means "put it now in a pre-determined place for attention at a later pre-decided time". If you decide to "delay", remember to come back to that group of items at a regular pre-determined interval.

- Every so often (at least monthly), take a look at your low priority items and deal with them quickly in one session. Clear them out in between times if a spare moment presents itself.

- Don't allow items to accumulate on your desktop, in your inbox or your in-tray. If you do this, you will find that you will waste much of your time rummaging. Do you want to appear like that dog in search of a bone?

Chapter 3 - Operacy

We are all familiar with the three Rs, Reading, wRiting and aRithmetic. Literacy and numeracy have been fundamental to learning through the ages. These skills have helped humanity progress from the cave to the stage which we have reached today. As has been said, we have moved from cave dwellers to astronauts.

Literacy and numeracy have helped propel us along the way. Another skill is vital to our continued development. For this, I have coined the term "operacy", the ability to move things along and get things done, the ability to see and work through potential obstacles to the conclusion of the task. We need to break the task down into manageable pieces and, yes, most importantly, finish the job.

Once I asked my daughter Bonnie to tell me about literacy numeracy and operacy. She successfully defined the first two, but she mistakenly understood the third as learning to sing. We laughed at the third definition, especially as Bonnie is herself a master in the field of operacy. It proved to me that you could be an expert at getting things done without necessarily knowing that your skill has a new name all of its own.

In our time, there is an urgent need for people to become skilled in operacy. Increasingly we have become a civilisation of people who cannot do things for ourselves. Electronics attend to many of our former mental gymnastics, and our physical exertions are increasingly for body maintenance rather than actual work. In this new world, we must work to retain the hands-on experience of doing things and building things.

Where we work with the aid of machines, we need to maintain our mental agility and see what we are doing, how we are doing it and why. And we must develop the ability to see the job through to its end.

In a world where our sports are becoming increasingly spectator events, we must retain the ability to participate actively ourselves. In those minutes standing to watch, we can and should, be inspired to believe that we can train ourselves to get up on our feet and take control of our affairs. It helps if we take time to exercise our minds and bodies regularly.

In work situations, management needs to act to enable their people rather than disable them. Helping people is a practice that works. Disabling people will always fail. Employees must be encouraged to have input into the product and be responsible for the final output quality. It is not easy to develop inspiration and creativity if you see yourself as a small cog in a giant wheel. If businesses are to be successful, they must develop their people and give employees a sense of pride in their contribution and participation.

Operacy means doing rather than simple planning. Planning is essential, but at some point, the planning needs to move into the stage of effective action leading through to completion. Operacy is concerned with progressing and finishing rather than simply starting. Of course, we must begin, and it is operacy that encourages us to begin. It inspires enthusiasm for the project. It incentivises people to take up the challenge and work to see a project through to its completion.

Operacy means getting things out of our heads. It means getting plans off the drawing board, iPad or tablet and into and out of the production line. It means getting the idea saved somewhere once the thought strikes in the first place. In horticultural terms, it means not only coming up with a garden design but digging the garden, planting, tending the plants and getting them to bloom. Operacy means using our energy, our drive, our enthusiasm and our technology to get something completed.

Operacy is concerned with the future, but it seeks to achieve the objective as soon as possible. It learns from the past but is mainly concerned with putting the present moment to good use to bring about the desired final result. Make the time to practice operacy this week.

Summary of this chapter:

- There are times when the planning must stop, and the work must begin and move on to a conclusion, in a word, operacy.

- Cultivate the desire to get things finished. Starting is necessary but is only a first step along the way to completion.

- Work with enthusiasm to turn your dreams into reality.

Chapter 4 - Grasp the nettle; it is less painful

In this chapter will get tips on how to avoid putting off an unpleasant task. You will learn how to become a person of action with results to your credit this week.

First, consider why we put off the difficult task. There are two main reasons which, between them, account for most cases of procrastination.

One - Paralysing doubt as to precisely what it is you have to do.

Two - The Fear of failure and the fear of making mistakes.

You remove the first of these excuses by careful consideration of the problem itself. It may be that there is a valid doubt as to how to tackle the project. But leaving it to simmer on the back burner will not help the task, bristling with difficulties though it may be.

You protest that you are not sure what to do. In that event, as a first step, you should seek assistance from someone qualified to give advice. It may be that there is more preliminary research to be done before you can logically tackle the project at all. Well then, go ahead and requisition that research now. Perhaps you need the approval of someone else. If so, seek that approval now.

It is essential to make a list of the preliminary points which are causing obstruction and take some action on each, delegating sections where appropriate. But do not delay the attack on the main task by engaging in more and more research. Once you have the preliminaries sorted, aim to get working on the project itself with the minimum delay. Remember the 80/20 rule when assembling these preliminaries. (See Chapter 16 - Pareto Principle) Why not get on with the job when you have Pareto's 80% of the research brought in from the first 20% of your effort?

You protest that more research is needed to ensure that you will be setting off on the right track. In this situation, remind yourself of the old saying, "the best can be the enemy of the good". Remember, if the preliminary research goes on forever, you will postpone the main task beyond time itself. You must get started sometime, so if you want to or need to get started, the sooner you begin, the better. Remember that to get any job completed, you reach a stage where the planning has to stop, and the action has to start.

Next, we look at the second obstacle, fear of failure. Fear of failure and fear of the possibility of mistakes can have a paralysing effect on a project unless you tackle these worries very firmly. There is only one way to ensure that you will never make a mistake, and that is never to try. And failure to try is undoubtedly the greatest mistake of all.

To help you overcome your fear of mistakes, consider these points:

An error, if it occurs at all, may be insignificant.

Even if significant, it may be reversible.

Even if significant and irreversible, it may be reparable.

Even if significant, irreversible and irreparable, it may not be calamitous.

If you continue on and on in that vein, it will bring you to this realisation: only a tiny percentage of mistakes, even when they do occur, result in some calamity.

Now look at your project again and ask yourself: What is the absolute worst thing that could happen to you if you try your best and you fail? Would you lose your life? Or your job? This thought should help you to keep matters in perspective when facing the fear of failure. And think of the other side. Think of the buzz that comes from the successful completion of any difficult task. Use these ideas to encourage you to make progress on one of your complex tasks this week.

Summary of this chapter:

• Realise that the unpleasant task will not go away on its own, so make it your business to tackle it now and put it behind you.

• Divide the task up, delegate any parts you can entrust to others, order the research, obtain the permissions and get on with it.

• Remember that there are very few fatal errors. The biggest and the only sure error is to fail to act at all.

Chapter 5 - Pros and cons lists - to do or not to do

Indecision paralyses action. Many projects languish on a shelf or sit in a notepad indefinitely. Sometimes they sit there fatally, for want of a clear decision as to what to do. Here is where a pros and cons list can help.

A list of pros and cons are your means of reaching decisions about your various options. Get into the habit of making decisions in this way, and your life will be less troubled by doubt and indecision. Remember that, almost certainly, the worst choice you can make is the choice to postpone a decision that you should make now.

Every day we make decisions which do not give rise to the need for anything as formal as a list of pros and cons. Often the right decision is obvious, and the balance in one direction or is so compelling that the question of weighing the advantages on either side does not arise. If you face easy decisions, get on with the job at making them and do not delay matters by postponing action and building up needless trouble. Your gut feeling will be right most of the time.

But at times there can appear to be several reasons which suggest you should do one thing and as many reasons why you should do the opposite. These situations call for a more formal approach if you want to find a rational decision with which you can live enthusiastically.

Your first step is to open a document, and on one side of the page, you will set out all the reasons which suggest you should make Decision A.

Do not attempt at this stage to evaluate the merits of any of the factors in support of Decision A. In this stage in the process, you are just searching for all the possible reasons you can find favouring Decision A.

Having completed your list of pros, then, in the same way, list all the reasons for Decision B. Do not begin with a preconceived prejudice as to the side of the fence on which you hope to land. Objectivity is the key when making your pros and cons list.

The next stage in the process is to examine the merits lying on either side of the argument. Any reasons which have little value or significance can, at this stage, be crossed off or deleted. By process of elimination, you will have some acceptably good reasons on either side.

This process will make it easier for you to reach a decision. If you have to make a choice, then you should base it on clear reasoning. That level-headed thinking will make it easier for you to live with whichever option you decide to make. You will avoid being troubled later on by any nagging feeling of self-doubt. The absence of doubt will help you build your determination to see the decision or project through to its conclusion.

Once you have made a decision, then make up your mind to be confident about it. Do not allow doubt to creep into the matter again. You have acquitted yourself of your first duty, which was the duty to decide. And you have come to a logical decision. For better or worse, you have made your choice. You have based it on rational consideration of the pros and cons. Now carry it through without hesitation. Remember to use the pros and cons system the next time you have a crucial decision to make.

Summary of this chapter:

- If you are faced with a decision, realise that the worst possible choice is to postpone making the decision. Some choices are easy. Make them without hesitation.

- For more weighty decisions, list the reasons for, the pros, and the reasons against, the cons. Weigh the merits of the respective arguments and decide.

- Once you have made the decision, leave the agonising behind you. Get on with the task, energised by the enthusiasm of one who has decided.

Chapter 6 - Decisions Please

You will have come across the saying, "the best is the enemy of the good". Sometimes you are faced with an important choice. You research, you seek advice, think, seek more advice, ponder, do some more research, and finally decide to... postpone the decision. But this process is the way to get things delayed, not the way to get things done.

In the affairs of life, you will frequently encounter a moment which we call decision time. Make the decision, and you will make progress and achieve success. Postpone the decision, and you will delay and perhaps destroy the prospect of success.

Now, you may say, such and such an undertaking is very weighty and needs careful consideration. This concern is a reasonable view. But remember, the matter finally needs a decision. And in a world of action, even a poor choice is better than none when a decision is required.

Some people are so fearful of making a mistake that they constantly postpone decision-making. By failing to come to a decision, they miss the opportunity to complete what might have proved to have been a valuable project. These are like death wishes. When they need to make a choice, these people actively seek out reasons for the postponement, and in doing so, they repeatedly shoot themselves in the foot.

When you have a critical judgment to make, you must give it due thought and consideration. That should take the form of seeking such advice as may be appropriate from someone qualified to provide you with it. Often research has to be done, data has to be collected, and you have to weigh up the consequences for and against each possible option. (See Chapter 5 - Pros and Cons lists) But incorporated into any agonising should be a definite time limit on the different stages of the pondering process and, most of all, a time limit for that vital moment of final decision making.

Sometimes there are logical and valid reasons for the postponement of decision-making. Problems and complexities may be such that a delayed decision is required. And, very occasionally, there are problems which solve themselves by the passage of time. The result of that situation is that you do not have to decide at all. But that opportunity for avoidance leading to a good outcome is rare. As a rule, delayed decision-making is not rationally justifiable, and delay tends to be indicative, not of the issue's scale, but rather the fear of making a mistake.

So the time has come, and you have made the decision. Have no regrets. Remember that even worse than any wrong decision is no decision at all. At worst, an erroneous decision will be a lesson that may have some application in the future. Failure to decide can offer the possibility that the problem will go away by itself, but that is not a lesson on which to base future non-decision-making. It only adds another brick in the wall of fear that, to some extent, surrounds us all in these matters, and it separates us from the success that awaits us when we step outside our comfort zone and make a decision.

When you have decided, accept your choice without regret and act upon it enthusiastically and without hesitation. Life and success belong to those who are willing to grasp the opportunity and live with the consequences of their decisions. If it helps, set out your conclusion (and the reasons for it) in permanent form. You will find this an aid in putting indecision behind you and getting on with the choice you have made.

If you attend a meeting and you find it dominated by uncertainty, let you be the catalyst for action. Ask, "and what have we decided to do?" and ask it again if necessary. Don't let the overcautious and the procrastinators take over a decision-making meeting.

Decide today to become a person who can be relied upon to come to a firm rational decision and live with the consequences. Take reasonable care, of course, but whatever you do, remember to decide. Most of the time, everything you carefully choose to do will turn out just fine.

Summary of this chapter:

- The worst possible decision is no decision at all.

- Seek advice, research, check, ponder, but above all, decide.

- Having decided, don't look back, be determined to live with the decision and its consequences and see it through.

Chapter 7 - Advance Planning

Have you ever set out without having made adequate planning and pre-checks? If so, you will have kicked yourself for arriving at the wrong hotel, even in the wrong city. It is like mindlessly travelling a long way to buy something in person without checking that what you are looking for is in stock at that particular location.

All this helps to demonstrate the need to plan and to save valuable time on fruitless activity. If you are travelling a long distance to meet someone, is it not prudent to check in advance to ensure that the person is still available and still has the appointment noted? This routine check only takes minutes, but what a potential time-saver it can be.

In the same way, it makes sense to book ahead for meals, for cinema and theatre tickets unless you are happy on occasion to head out with no particular destination in mind. The latter is alright if you wish to drop the planning and let events take their course. It can make a welcome change from the rigidity of having a fixed schedule for every occasion, but it is not the everyday way of getting things done.

Even with the benefit of satellite navigation, a little route checking in advance will save lots of time and frustration on the trip. It is not a relaxing experience to navigate unfamiliar territory as you drive along and makes sense, therefore, instead to give reasonable thought in advance. Can you arrange for someone to drive you? This aid is not a luxury enjoyed only by top executives. It may be possible to organise this at a little comparative expense, and you can save time and money by getting on with practical work along the way.

Just as it is important to check ahead before setting out, it is no joy to cut your transfer time so tight as to make insufficient allowance for delays. To avoid unnecessary stress and worry, you must build some spare time into your schedule so that you will have a reasonably relaxed preparation time ahead of meeting times and deadlines.

Be prepared for delays that are part and parcel of life. Have material and notes accessible so that otherwise lost time can be recouped. But do not depend upon delays arising along the way to prepare for the important business of your trip.

Delays happen when you least expect them, it is true, but you will also find that sometimes hoped-for delays do not arise at the very time when you need them. Life is just like that. So, like any boy scout or girl guide, be prepared. Spare time seldom arrives when you need it.

So, what can you get done if delays happen to occur? There will be no shortage of things you can usefully do in a world of instant communication and remote access. But why not simply relax and do nothing in these moments of gained time? And if you feel that this is a waste of time, consider this: sometimes just giving your mind a chance to allow some ideas to bubble up from your subconscious can itself be a beneficial exercise. So, if you get a chance to do so, why not simply let your mind wander over the range of your activities in a relaxed way.

When you begin to use delays in this way, you will find the stress factor immediately eases. Somehow the delays do not appear so troublesome when you come to realise that you have some inbuilt way of making use (or deliberate non-use) of the "lost" time.

When travelling, make sure to remain in communication. You need be to be contactable and stoppable if there is a last-minute change of plan. Suppose you decide to put your phone to sleep mode to have a break; remember to un-sleep your phone as soon as the break time is over.

Most important of all, it would be best if you did not embark on a business trip unless you cannot achieve the same result by way of a remote meeting.

Summary of this chapter:

•   Take time to plan your route before you set off on a trip, first asking yourself if the trip is essential. Do you need to be physically present for this meeting?

•   Have something in mind to do (or not to do) if you encounter a delay, but plan to arrive with more than enough time to spare.

•   Do not depend upon spare time arising. Make sure you remain contactable in case of last-minute changes or cancellations.

Chapter 8 - Divide and Conquer

Do you know that you can divide every seeming impossibility into several steps, each of which is possible? It may not be possible to overcome a significant obstacle in one full frontal assault, but by dividing it up, you can surmount even the most daunting problem.

Where do you begin, and how do you muster up the strength to start? Faced with a complex problem and without having developed the habit advocated in this chapter, everything within you will encourage you to delay and postpone the task. There are as many excuses for inactivity as there are people and problems avoiding each other. But begin, you must. So why not this week?

The first thing you must do is take some step, any step, in the desired direction. Tell yourself that you will devote 10 minutes, not working on the problem itself, but only on the preliminaries. In that time, you will divide the problem into its constituent parts.

You will find to your surprise that, however daunting the overall task may be, there will be little difficulty gaining the courage and energy to make out this preliminary list. You have made a pact with yourself that, for now, you are only concerned with setting out the subdivisions of the task. You are not obliged to take the matter any further today.

Set out the overall objective and list, item by item, the matters requiring attention to achieve that aim. Opposite each item, it will be helpful to note how you should attend to it and when. For some aspects, you will find that the subdivision is suitable for delegation or requires activity or input on the part of someone else. But do not be tempted at this stage to go off on that tangent. Remember your pact with yourself. This first stage is to break down the problem into manageable chunks and not work on it as such.

It will be found as a rule that the breaking down of the task in this way is sufficient to dispel any paralysing cloud of uncertainty and anxiety which has attached to the job. Primarily the doubt and delay will have arisen from fear of the unknown. Added to this will be your concern about the now long-neglected nature of the task. Sometimes it will be found that the dreaded obstacles preventing you from starting the project are nothing at all compared to the problems that have arisen because of the delay. After this divide and conquer exercise, you are now dealing with a known and now less neglected project.

Having spent 10 minutes in this beneficial activity, you will likely have gained momentum sufficient to encourage you to continue in the same vein. Stage one, the essential breakdown, is complete. You may decide that a little more time is required to break down the project further. In that situation, you may choose to continue. Whether you agree to the extension of time to enable you to continue to work on the division today is a matter for yourself.

When trying to overcome a severe inertia problem, the vital first assault must never be tainted with the numbing idea that you must continue after the designated first period agreed with yourself. There is no need to press on at this point unless you genuinely feel the urge to do so. We are encouraging here the application of a simple and guaranteed painless first stage. When you complete this early stage, you will be less likely to refuse to tackle the next phase of even the most daunting task.

You may gain such heart on the breaking down of a project in this way that you will want to continue to make progress this very day. If so, that is fine. You will see many small actions that can be taken at once or might be suitable for delegation to someone else. Suddenly you find that on several fronts, you are progressing a task that was at a standstill. You will find that your train begins to move along the track. Just as in the case of a train, you will need less energy to keep moving along. You have learnt to divide and conquer. You have remembered to drop the word "impossible" from your dictionary and your mind. Congratulations.

But just before you leave the project for today, make a summary of what you should do next. That will make it less daunting to return to the matter tomorrow, and it will get you off to a quicker start when you do return.

Summary of this chapter:

- Almost every seeming impossibility can be divided into several steps, each of which is possible.

- Take 10 minutes to set your problem down and set out the different steps you need to take to progress it.

- Remember, doubt paralyses action. When you subdivide the job, you will have removed much of that uncertainty, and you can progress the project more easily

Chapter 9 - Delegate or Suffocate

If the work to be done exceeds one individual's capacity to do it, there is a need to delegate. So, it is necessary to stress the importance of timely and appropriate delegation.

Why delegate?

1.   unless you learn to delegate, the work you have to get through will slow down in a bottleneck of your own making,

2.   If you fail to trust and delegate, the people on your team will never understand the processes involved in your operation and how to get on with the work themselves. This further increases your workload, making the thought of holidays or free time something you will dread.

3.   You can increase your output capacity directly in proportion to your ability and willingness to delegate.

4.   Remember that there are only so many hours in the week. If you want to overcome the limits which these hours place on your output, you must learn to delegate ahead of crises.

5.   If you fail to delegate, you will have to complete the job single-handedly and inefficiently when the deadline hits (and it will).

So why won't you delegate?

1. You don't have the time to explain the job. But the time saved by timely delegation will far outweigh the time spent in one-off explanations, especially when repetitive tasks are in issue.

2. You fear that other people will not be able to do the work as well as you. That may be so but is it not time other people learned these skills for their sakes as well as your own?

3. You fear that people may make mistakes. But equally, errors may be made by you if you are missing deadlines and working under increased pressure which you add to every time you fail to delegate.

4. You fear becoming answerable for the work of other people. But you are answerable anyway. Can you not exercise appropriate control and guidance over your people in the same way you receive proper advice and guidance when you are assigned something?

So, what to do this week about delegation:

Take a look at Chapter 13 (to-do list) and Chapter 20 (action-sorter) to consider which of the tasks listed for attention there might be suitable for delegation now.

Have confidence in the ability of your people to use their intelligence and skill. If you have tasks suitable for delegation, delegate them now. Give appropriate directions and fix the limit of the authority delegated.

Give an outline of the circumstances in which the person concerned should refer back to you for clearance or guidance. But do not encourage reverse delegation, or you will find yourself taking back a delegated task. This ever-present possibility must be discouraged.

If the delegated tasks are only a tiny part of the whole, give the people concerned sufficient information to enable them to see where this task fits into the general scheme of things.

Avoid spoon-feeding the person to whom the task has been delegated. It is better for the person to understand the result you want to achieve rather than have them mindlessly following some set of procedures. A group of clearly defined methods can help limit duplication of effort and unnecessary relearning in certain circumstances. But, to be effective, the person needs to feel ownership of the task.

Delegate meaningful tasks, not just the ones you find unpleasant. And avoid delegating tasks that you are unsure about, such as new processes and critically essential functions that you may be nervous about tackling yourself. Delegation is a way of getting the work done more effectively; it is not an excuse for pushing an unpleasant or dubious problem out to another person.

Consider delegating tasks that you find particularly easy. Remember that you may be using these routine activities as an excuse for delaying attending to more important tasks that you are postponing because you are unsure how to tackle them.

Make it your aim to set up guidelines for different subdivisions of your work so that what you fear delegating today will at least be suitable for delegation tomorrow or next week. You must trust people in this respect or drown in a sea of overwork.

Summary of this chapter:

- If the work exceeds your capacity as an individual, you must delegate part of it.

- If you fail to delegate you will set yourself up as indispensable and you will find it impossible to be absent from work until one day you....

- Delegate meaningful tasks and not simply items that you dread doing yourself. Remember to delegate routine tasks that you may be doing yourself as an excuse for your own procrastination on more complex but more meaningful work.

Chapter 10 – Project Post Mortem

Do you fear holding a post-mortem following the conclusion of a project? Are you fearful that such sessions have, in the past, been witch-hunts designed to lay the blame for any failed aspects once a suitably compliant scapegoat has been identified and cornered?

Fear not, because what I propose here is a creative project post-mortem to note the lessons learned from the project and to lay down helpful guidelines for those who have to organise something of a similar nature in the future.

One of the notable differences between humans and animals is our ability to communicate. Employing communication and language, we have custody of an ever-increasing common fund of knowledge that can pass, not just between us present here but between one generation and the next.

Similarly, but on a more local level, there is in all our organisations and businesses the ability to build up a set of experiences. You can use these to avoid constantly have to waste time and energy reinventing any particular wheel.

By carrying out a practical project post-mortem after the conclusion of a project, we can see that one team's labours are not lost as far as other people are concerned. We can ensure that the experience gained and lessons learned survive intact for our future benefit.

Remember that it is unnecessary to add to the build-up of paper and computer files by keeping meticulous records of all the minutiae of every single part of every project undertaken. But some situations and cases are of such usefulness and frequency of occurrence that we should record the lessons learned. These notes will benefit those who are likely to encounter the same or similar situations in the future.

Records kept as a result of a project post-mortem should show how and why you undertook the project, the steps taken, the specific good features and any pitfalls encountered, and the lessons learned. It will help if you retain clear notes which will assist in avoiding any such pitfalls arising in the future.

It will also be helpful to note here, who helped with this project, the outside sources to which the organisation had to have recourse, how reliable those sources were, and whether they should be looked to again if a similar situation were to arise in the future.

Where will the records of this event be held? How will you be able to locate the information next time around? Is there a computer record or pathname that will help anyone easily access the knowledge the next time they need it? A little time spent now in a practical project post-mortem will save considerable time when an operation of this type arises in the future.

You will see that this type of post-mortem, project learning by reference to project doing, is far from the fearful witch-hunt that is frequently the stuff of post-project meetings. Such with-hunts are the reason for the avoidance of potentially useful discussions after an event.

We are all wiser after the event, and even a failure today can help provide lessons leading to more success tomorrow.

We neglect project post-mortems at our peril. So much time and energy will have gone into a first-of-a-kind project. It is crucial to capture experiences and lessons while they are fresh in our minds. To miss out on the chance to preserve this working experience for the future represents a significant waste of time. Avoiding a project post-mortem is to bury one's head in the sand, believing, hoping, that a project like this will never arise again. When it does, it finds you unprepared, and off you go reinventing the wheel—what a great pity that is, and what an awful waste of your time.

Summary of this chapter:

- Build up a valuable store of knowledge by holding a project post mortem to conclude any significant project.

- This is not a witch-hunt. The aim is improvement next time around. You want to avoid having to reinvent the wheel.

- Ensure that you can easily find the notes and records the next time a similar project arises.

Part 3 – Organising Yourself

One way to organize your thoughts is to tidy up, even if it is in places where it makes no sense at all.

-    *Ursus Wehrli*

Chapter 11 – Lark or Owl – Finding Your Optimum Time

Do you prefer to rise with the larks or work with the owls? Have you figured out your optimum time of day?

Are you the sort of person who rises enthusiastically to greet each new day? Or would you class yourself as someone who finds it hard to get going in the morning but who can maintain and increase your momentum when the larks have succumbed to the call of the night?

It is essential to know your optimum time for creative and energetic work and organise your schedule accordingly.

Try out a few different routines and see which of them works best for you. Most people assume they need eight hours of sleep a night, and many do need that amount of sleep to work effectively. But you will have heard accounts of many people who claim to get by effectively on less sleep than this. Adequate sleep is essential for our health.

I suggest you begin by getting up earlier for a week or two. Do not expect to make a rational assessment after only a day or two of this experiment. It will take you a little while to adjust. Try to get into an active mode early and if you must travel for work, see that you travel when you expect to encounter less traffic. If that does not suit your particular job, try to use that early morning period for some creative activity. Examine your effectiveness after a couple of weeks and note any lessons you may have learnt from your earlier start.

Next, you might experiment with a later start and a later finish. See how it suits you to use time late at night for creative activity. See if the inspiration flows after midnight, or do you notice that your ability to work effectively dries up as the night proceeds. If the creativity still flows, you may find that you are at one with the owls.

If your work routine allows you the possibility of experimentation, try to take a short nap in the middle of the day and see what effect that has on your energy levels. It is not necessary (and hardly practical) that you return to bed, although some people manage to do just that. A simple lie back in your chair, or in your car, or someplace where you can relax in your place of work is sufficient. You may at first need or wish to try out some relaxation recordings to set the atmosphere, but after a while and as the routine takes hold, you will find it easy to drift into a state of relaxation without the need for any such aid.

The purpose of all this is to experiment with and get to assess your body clock. By doing so, you will understand your inner timing systems to be able to harness them and put them to use most effectively.

After some experimentation, you will find out whether you are a lark or an owl. If a lark, you should try to allocate the early part of your day for your most important and productive activities. You would be surprised to see the number of people who waste their mornings routinely reading the news headlines, routinely checking emails, checking post and generally attending to things in the order in which they happen to hit. These same people find themselves running out of steam later in the day. Consequently, they find themselves postponing to an indefinite tomorrow those things that require a high concentration of energy.

Each tomorrow comes equipped with its supply of routine post and emails to be looked at and daily headlines for reading. People who spend their mornings routinely attending to things in the order in which they happen to hit can find themselves dangerously delaying essential tasks.

Owls should deliberately allocate their creative work to the later hours that best suit their personalities and internal clocks. Their days begin slowly with everyday items just about bearable. Still, as the owls gain momentum, their energy levels soar and finally, owls hit their most creative and energy peak long after larks have retired for the night.

This chapter's advice is that you learn to read your internal body clock and put it to use for your benefit. Don't try to cheat your body clock. It knows best.

Summary of this chapter:

- Experiment with your timetable and your activities to determine if you are a lark or an owl.

- Use your most energetic time for your most important work.

- Don't fritter away your most energetic time on trivia.

Chapter 12 - A place for everything

One of the cornerstones of your system will be to find a logical place for everything. You must work to keep everything, papers, electronic data, all things, in locations where you can find them quickly when required.

This principle is a straightforward idea, but it can hardly ever be practised enough either in a work or a home situation. Just consider the inundation of material coming in and think of the time you may have lost in recent days or weeks trying to find something you did not allocate to a place where you would expect to find it. This rule applies to everything we need to store and find. It applies to electronic information, papers, documents and notes as well as material things.

No doubt you will have heard it argued by some people that it is a waste of time trying to keep things in their place. But we do not have an alternative if we wish to operate productively. Consider the downsides of working and living in a permanent state of disorder and confusion. Now, of course, we are human beings, not robots, and at times the situation in front of any of us will drift out of control. But the re-establishment of order is essential if we wish to get anything done with ease or efficiency.

This week make an investment that will give you repeated gains every day in the future. Find a logical place for everything, including electronic records and decide to keep everything in its own place.

People have been predicting the end of paper for a very long time. Yes, we operate in an increasingly paperless world, but many situations give rise to writing and written notes. You must deal with this paperwork.

Follow the directions contained in Chapter 14 – (Clear your Clutter) to get your papers into logical order to ensure that they can be stored, found and recovered when necessary.

When applying the advice contained here in this chapter, make sure that you establish the physical systems needed to store your material in some logical way. Do you have sufficient shelves, baskets, folders and cabinets so that papers and material things can be logically held, divided, positioned and easily found? Is everything labelled and indexed, not only for your benefit but so that other people who need to do so may also have easy access to these items in your absence?

Is your physical equipment logically laid out? Are the most commonly used items kept nearest at hand, or do you find you have to run to another room even for a piece of sticky tape? Are the notes, precedents, handbooks, and guidelines that you need easily accessible either physically or electronically in your work situation? The more frequently these items are required, the more critical it is for you to find them easily.

These thoughts will prompt questions of your own. Only you can devise a system for the organisation of your own life and work. Every person is unique. You will find people who enjoy having things arranged in an organised way. Other individuals are less so.   But the application of the general rule is beneficial for all of us.   There must be a place for everything. There should be no scurrying through a bundle of disorganised papers to find something that you have temporarily left in some unremembered place. Similarly, there should be no flustered searching through emails and computer records to find something that ought to be in its own easily remembered location.

You will make constant gains in time by faithfully applying the ideas contained in this chapter. Once having established a system, make sure that it is not allowed to fall apart. Nothing should take up residence in your home or office without it having been allocated to an appropriate place. You may allow yourself a small quarantine area for unallocated incoming paper or electronic materials. But the right of residence there should be severely restricted. Remind yourself to clear that area regularly. Keep a reminder about this someplace where you can periodically monitor it.

Summary of this chapter:

- You will lose a lot of time by rummaging for misplaced items that are of no fixed abode. These can be electronic records as well as papers and material things.

- Have a place for everything and keep everything in its place. This rule is not a counsel of perfection but of necessity.

- Have a short-term storage area for items on the move. Clear that area at regular intervals to keep everything in its place. If you find yourself having to rummage, this is a reminder that it is time to clear the area.

Chapter 13 - Don't go without a To-Do list

You may have heard it said if you do not know where you are headed, you are likely to arrive somewhere else—expressed in another way that is the saying that if you don't know where you are going any road will bring you there. A to-do list is how you will set a direction for your work. Without this aid, your work will depend upon the whim of the moment. Interruptions, important and unimportant, will gain precedence over every plan, with trivia gaining ground over lifetime significant projects.

If there is one thing sure about organisational methods, you have to believe this one. Without organising your plans into some form of a to-do list, you will never work consistently to achieve your objectives. In trying to gain time, keep a clear desk, decide priorities, break a complex project into manageable parts; for all of these, you must have a to-do list.

In its simplest form, a to-do list is an unsorted list, preferably visible at a glance, on one page showing everything which currently requires your attention. The key to operating such a plan is simplicity. The more detailed the list is, the less likely you will be to trouble yourself with it. In setting up a to-do list it helps if you indicate the relative importance of the items listed in a very preliminary way.

When you note something as needing your attention, you add it immediately to your to-do list. If it is relatively significant, you should highlight it in some way. I would highly recommend that you not revert to keeping the information relevant to the item on your desk or desktop. If a paper is involved, it should be in its place and only taken out when you are working upon it. The list is a means of keeping your desk or worktop clear of distractions as you work on the listed items one at a time in order of their priority. As you clear each item, you have the satisfaction of striking it off your list. Even if you have not cleared your list entirely at the end of the day, you will possess the happy feeling of having achieved something definite and in some order of priority.

Remember to develop the habit of always adding a new matter to the list before working on that incoming matter. The plan is that your to-do list becomes your framework for action. It makes no sense to have a list if you revert to the old ways and begin working on new activities without reference to what you have already decided requires attention. Do not be disturbed or disheartened if you do not get all the listed items cleared every day or even any day. You can carry forward items if necessary.

Advantages of a to-do list:

1. The list rather than some stand-alone note or paper reminds you of what you need to do.

2. Without the aid of a to-do list, you will be tempted to keep everything requiring attention on your desk, which will quickly turn into the quicksand of which all disordered desks are an example. It is true, placing items there in the first instance is done with the best of good intentions, but next, you will find that something else arrives for the desk or desktop just as the phone rings, and you have to take another note. You must keep your work area clear and rely on your to-do list to remind you of what needs your attention.

3.   You can keep your to-do list with you and may have an opportunity to reprioritise if you find you have time to spare by arriving too early for an outside appointment.

In Chapter 20 – (Action-Sorter), you will see some helpful ideas for developing a still more advantageous form of the to-do list. And as you get used to the discipline, it will become second nature to have your list made out in that even better format. But assuming you do not already operate a list system, the first step will be to establish the routine of having a simple item by item list to gain control over your projects and maintain an uncluttered desktop, worktop, and mind.

Summary of this chapter:

•   Do not keep unsorted notes on your desk or cluttered desktop as a way of attempting to remember what it is that you need to do.

•   Keep the items themselves where they belong and use a to-do list to remind you of the matters that require your attention.

•   Highlight the items of particular importance. When you have mastered the art of working from a to-do list, move on to the suggestions contained in Chapter 20 – (Action-Sorter), to gain even more control over your priorities.

Chapter 14 – Clear your Clutter day

In his book Clear your Desk, Declan Tracy encourages each organisation to have an annual "clear your desk" day. This suggestion is an excellent idea worthy of implementation in every organisation. In all businesses, there is a tendency for clutter to pile up. Often, the custodians of paper mountains and the electronic equivalent believe that they are too busy to clear their own areas. This belief is a false idea and a mistaken view.

We would all agree that a clear desk is a good idea. But when it comes to practice, we seem to believe that it is everyone else's desk that should be cleared. We have to work to bring about the conviction that this is a job for "me too" and not just an idea and an ideal for someone else.

It is impossible to organise anything effectively in a condition of clutter. Whether paper or electronic, chaos always has the effect of preventing you from seeing the main task needing your attention. E-mails in an inbox, documents, notes and files piled at random will each call for your attention many times before you finally get around to giving any of them the attention they need. It is essential to clear your clutter.

If an organisation can establish a "clear your clutter day", then all personnel can be encouraged to participate at the same time. If all are working together to pursue the same objective, everyone will more easily overcome their natural reluctance to deal with the mess. Besides, the fact that everyone will occupy themselves on the same task will reduce internal interruptions on the chosen day. Colleagues and workmates will each be too busy dealing with their own clutter to be able to find time to distract you from your clearance operation.

When you fix a day for this exercise, let everyone participate with enthusiasm and energy. This call for participation applies to people at the top, the newest comer and everyone in between. We can all do with improvement in this area. Even those who are practitioners of a no-clutter policy will find ideas to further perfect their clutter management.

The policy on such a clearance day should be deliberately liberal. "If in doubt, throw it out" should be the starting off point. There should be no escape for memos, papers and notes in the category "might be useful someday". Naturally a genuinely valuable document should be allocated to a place where you would expect to find it.

You need to set guidelines, of course, so that critical legal or other difficult-to-replace documents will not be thrown out with the trash. But generally, the problem will be the opposite, with plenty of duplicated copies sitting on files just waiting for someone to take the initiative and dispatch them to a physical or electronic bin.

It is essential to note the need for confidentiality regarding some items. When dealing with paper, you must distinguish between documents that must go for shredding and non-confidential written material, which you may discard without that need. Keep in mind also our responsibility to the environment to ensure that anything recyclable is recycled.

Computers have not brought about the promised paperless society, and the paper mountain still tends to grow exponentially. You should take care to delete duplicated files and copies. Nevertheless, you must set reasonable guidelines, so you do not delete anything of importance.

Remember the need to clear useless and duplicate data and redundant documents from your computer system. Unless you maintain order in your electronic records, it will be difficult and hopelessly time-consuming to locate what you need when you need it. A clear desk day must deal with any untidiness in your computer records also. Remember the importance of keeping routine, reliable and verified backups that can be accessed when required. All systems break down eventually, so you should be prepared for that eventuality.

Summary of this chapter:

- Organise a clear your clutter day annually to overcome the problem of clutter systematically.

- "If in doubt, throw it out ", but take care with legal and vital records. You do not want to drown in a sea of confusion, but you must use your head also.

- Clear clutter from your computer system too, and remember to carefully keep periodic backups that can be accessed when the need arises (it will).

Chapter 15 - Parkinson's Law

It is true; the work will expand to fill the time available for its completion. Put another way, so long as you feel you have an indefinite amount of time to spend on a project, you will find there will never be enough time for you to do all you think you need to do.

We all know of highly productive people in work, people who could not wait to reach the age of retirement so they could finally do all the things they ever dreamt of doing. Along comes the much-anticipated day, and in a short while, the retired person is unable to find the time to send an e-mail, write a letter or post a card. This happening is not a universal experience, but when it happens, you can place the reason firmly within the operation of Parkinson's Law. When the time was short, we had much to do and little time in which to do it. The energy was high, and output was high to match. Suddenly, there is less to be done and much more time in which to do it. We reduce our expectations, take things more easily, and slowly we begin to miss targets. We take things more easily, more slowly, and, true to Parkinson's Law, our output drops significantly.

Parkinson's Law applies to materials as well as to time. It operates at home as well as at work. Unchecked, the papers and files will continually expand to fill the vacant spaces in presses and cabinets. The data and computer files will always tend to expand to fill the available storage space. Have you ever seen a kitchen press empty? Why not be the one to stop the application of Parkinson's in your home and your place of work?

The way forward is to introduce meaningful deadlines for the amount of time devoted to particular projects. This deadline should apply whether it is simply reading the news headlines, studying a textbook, or completing a big project. This approach encourages us to take sensible shortcuts. It promotes delegation and ensures that we get on with the tasks on hand most simply and efficiently.

How can work be speeded up and tackled more efficiently? All of us have experienced the answer. Just think of the week (and the day) before you set off on holidays. You want to, and you need to leave everything in good order. So you delegate, you short-circuit, you vigorously push and shove to move matters along. I imagine most of us manage to get the work of two weeks or more done in the final days before the holidays. We know we can do it when there is a need to do it.

So, why do we not approach our affairs in this manner every week? Enter Parkinson's Law. We have more time, so we take more time. We will be here tomorrow, so we feel that we can safely postpone matters until tomorrow. We will be here next week, so we believe we can leave tasks on the long finger. The element of urgency has gone, and with it has disappeared our ability to see a target clearly and to head straight for it.

With the deadline removed, out with it has gone the need to implement the shortcuts that would have enabled us to meet it (had we set a deadline in the first place). We are not under pressure, so we don't delegate, we don't speed read, we don't use shortcuts to efficiency. This practice (or non-practice) is the tendency to inertia that we have to work to overcome.

So would it not be a good idea to live each week, not as if it were our last week, but at least as if it were the week before our holidays? If we are people who get a burst of energy for completion on a Friday, let us act as if every day was a Friday. Let us motivate ourselves to work as if all depended on our getting this job completed by a self-imposed deadline, and let us set a deadline to encourage ourselves along.

The gained momentum will be noticed by everyone if we try, as we should, to reduce the operation of Parkinson's Law in a business situation. The idea of delegating will become normal; we will twist circles and curves into straight lines, and we will all become more productive. You can work on this idea this week, even tomorrow, as if tomorrow was the day just before your holidays.

Summary of this chapter:

- The work will expand to fill the time available. The materials will expand to fill the vacant storage areas. Avoid this happening by setting limits.

- Fix limits in terms of space, introduce deadlines in terms of time to help encourage matters along without the delays arising from excessive perfectionism.

- Approach your work today as if you are going on holidays tomorrow.

Chapter 16 - The Pareto Principle - Avoid Perfectionism

Named after the Italian economist and sociologist Alfredo Pareto (1848-1923), this is also known as the 80/20 rule. In any given group, the theory is that approximately 20% will be of overwhelming significance, and the remaining 80% (even taken together) will be of much less importance. Advocates of the rule will tell you that 20% of customers account for 80% of the profits. They will advise you that the first 20% of effort produces 80% of the result, that 80% of our knowledge comes from 20% of our sources.

Whether the theory is capable of absolute scientific proof is unimportant. What is relevant to understand is in that considering any given number of matters requiring attention, a comparative few (for argument, let us agree 20%) will be more significant. Followers of the theory believe that this 20% accounts for 80% of the result. The remaining 20% will be of little comparative value accounting for only 20% of the outcome.

You need to go no further than your back garden to realise the usefulness of the 80/20 approach to your work. As you organise youself to restore that area after a winter of neglect, it is abundantly clear that the first 20% of your time and effort will produce 80% of the improvement. So why would you spend that initial effort multiplied by four to yield only your first output divided by four? Why should you work most of your time at 1/16 of your optimum productivity? It is easy to see how applying the Pareto Principle can dramatically improve your effectiveness.

You can put this principle into effect in your life this week with beneficial effect. The 80/20 rule is a firm reminder of the fruitlessness of over perfectionism. The theory can cut away unnecessary finishing touches, which will make only the slightest difference to the result. Remember that you will complete 80% of your task quite adequately by employing the first 20% of your time and effort and without the perfectionist finishing touches that absorb the remaining 80% of your effort and time.

Not many of us are operating in situations requiring an absolute (or near absolute as can be found) level of perfectionism. Most of us are not charged with the task of controlling or maintaining aircraft or spacecraft, or nuclear power stations.

Ask if the 80/20 question has application in your life and, if it has, then concentrate your efforts on the aspects that will bring about significant results in proportion to your effort.

If you face a cluttered desk or desktop, realise the 20% of the material will be of more significant importance. Concentrate on pinpointing that 20% and attend to that now, leaving the less significant 80% for attention later (if at all). See Chapter 2 – (Do, Dump, Delegate or Delay).

If you consider that for 20% of your day, you will be at your peak performance, try to use the time of day when your energy levels will be at their highest and concentrate your important projects for these times. Some of us are larks with energy levels at their height at daybreak. Others are owls who are at their best when the larks are only fit for bed. Find your optimum time and use it for optimum effect.

Suppose you are embarking on a sales campaign, consider that 20% of the target group will probably account for 80% of the result. Therefore, try to target your efforts accordingly. If you are dealing with existing clients, examine your records and not neglect the 20% of people who deliver 80% of your profits.

When you look at this book, or any book, first examine how it can help you by first taking a look at the subjects covered. Then, knowing your weaknesses and strengths, consider which 20% of the content can be put more usefully into effect right now, giving you 80% of the value of the entire book for only 20% of your time and effort.

Summary of this chapter:

• Avoid perfectionism. The best can be the enemy of the good.

• Remember that the first 20% of your effort will produce 80% of the result.

• Be aware that the remaining 80% of your time and effort will only deliver the remaining 20% of the result.

Chapter 17 – Appointments

One key to the organisation of your life's time will be the systematic keeping of your appointment diary. Many of us do not enjoy the luxury of having a personal assistant, but you may just be lucky to have that assistance in your particular work situation. Quite apart from the time saved by having an assistant attend to the appointment details, it will be much easier for an assistant to diplomatically arrange the appointment to slot into some pre-planned logical time sequence.

In planning your work, you must try to retain every week some periods for unbroken attention to matters requiring special concentrated care. Your plan should be to organise appointments in groups of their own so that you will not find your days peppered with booked interruptions to the aspects of your work that require unbroken thought.

It should be politely explained to visitors that you aim to keep your appointments, and you need visitors to do the same. Without appearing arrogant, impress on visitors the importance of coming to a meeting armed with relevant information. Many people seek advice without having to hand all the relevant papers and information fundamental to the problem on which advice is being sought.

It will be helpful if you arrange your appointments in blocks. In this way, one consultation or interview will help push the others along, and there will be less opportunity for extended periods of small talk. This small talk is a valuable aspect of life, and it helps lubricate our relationships. Still, there is a need for some limitation in work situations and a little more emphasis on getting done what needs doing.

Similarly, if people have an appointment with you, you should not leave them waiting. Therefore, prospective visitors should discuss and try to agree on the amount of time they require for any appointment.

A helpful practice is to organise appointments for those times of day when your enthusiasm and energy might otherwise flag. Owls may benefit from offering morning appointments, which will help wake them up and get the day off to a quick start. Larks might find that afternoon appointments provide the extra stimulus they need to keep going when they might otherwise be beyond their most productive hours.

It would be best if you tried to arrange appointments, as far as possible, to facilitate the needs of the visitors. A different time slot for each day of the week might be one way to ensure that people who need to see you will always be able to meet you at a time of day which suits them.

It is sensible to establish the principle that people coming in late for appointments will not be allowed to inconvenience those who arrive on time. If X is scheduled for 15:00 hours and appears at 15:20, you should diplomatically explain your policy whereby people do not have to wait for appointments. Suppose the latecomer wishes to see you today. In that case, it will be a matter of them hoping for some cancellation or another late arrival or that you might briefly deal with the issue in a gap arising between some later appointments.

It is important to always prepare yourself fully for your meetings. You must anticipate the matters which you need to address. If you expect to give a progress report on something, make sure to equip yourself with the relevant information well in advance. Do not place reliance on having minutes between one appointment and the next to prepare for that following appointment. It never works out that way, nor would it be wise to work on that basis.

If people have an appointment with you, you must always deal with them in a friendly, competent and professional manner. Any meeting should end (a) without time having been wasted, (b) with information exchanged and (c) clear strategies agreed upon as to the following steps to be taken and by whom.

Summary of this chapter:

- If possible, in your work situation, have your appointments arranged by an assistant. Try to ensure that people, when they meet with you, come equipped with the relevant information.

- Organise appointments in groups to allow yourself a better opportunity for those necessary unbroken periods for concentrated work.

- To obtain the maximum benefit from the meeting, ensure that you are always well prepared for your appointments.

Chapter 18 – Interruptions

They affect us all, the constant stream of interruptions that seem to deflect us from our intended work. These happenings can be an actual irritation until we realise that necessary, as distinct from trivial, interruptions can fuel our activities' fire.

Think of it this way. If we were to plod along without interruption or stimulus, we would likely fall asleep for want of stimulation. Interruptions concentrate the mind regardless of how they arise. Their messages need to be classified and prioritised, and they force us to note our position and adjust our sights to remain on target while still taking the interruption into account as necessary.

But we need a system for directing the interruptions into stimulants which can improve our productivity. If what you are working on is critically important, it would be foolhardy to drop that project, favouring the first interruption that beckons. But the interruption itself may remind you that you have another task that you must note for attention in its proper order of priority. You must return to the critical project on hand accompanied by a renewed determination to remain faithfully on the track you have set yourself.

It would be essential to avoid a tendency to switch tasks in response to random interruptions. If you do so, you will get nothing done effectively; you will dissipate your energy like a boxer responding to a pounding. At the end of the working day, you will feel as if you have accomplished nothing definite, even though you may have been busy running from one job to another all day long. It would be best if you arrange in your schedule blocks of unbroken time for concentrated work.

In your system, you need to find a place where you can systematically record matters for attention arising from any interruptions which may come your way. We switch tasks in reply to interruptions because we fear that we will forget the new assignment unless we immediately dispose of it. Suppose for a moment that we have a reliable system for taking note of matters requiring attention in order of priority. In that case, there will be no such danger, and the critical work on hand can be proceeded with without any fear that we will forget the incoming matter. Please see the advice in Chapter 13 - (To-Do lists).

Face-to-face interruptions can be of two kinds. You may have colleagues who need assistance or customers or clients requiring attention. We cannot afford to ignore either, but it should be possible to arrange a workable system to assist colleagues needing help which will not leave you subject to an unsettling barrage of their random interruptions. Could you agree that people should approach you with their problems (if any) at a particular time of the day? It makes no sense that people are interrupting you randomly and perhaps for trivial reasons, which, in the process, interrupts your concentration.

But remember, we are here thinking positively of interruptions. Is there a lesson for you in the frequency nature of the intrusion? Why do your colleagues look to you for advice or direction so often? Has this to do with their training? Are they unsure of what to do? Or is it a matter of your holding on too tightly to control so that people have to have your blessing for every little thing? You know what happens to a bottle under pressure if the neck is too small. The answer is simple; it bursts. Give thought to the level of delegation and the extent of authority passed down the line so that your people will not need such spoon-feeding.

You must never consider customers and clients as interruptions to your "normal" work. Customers are the reason for the existence of your business. If you wish to serve them effectively and succeed in your business, there can be no way your customers can be looked upon or thought of as trouble. You must look upon each customer interaction as a window of opportunity, a moment of truth. If a customer requires attention, ensure that the customer gets attention there and then from someone qualified to satisfy them. No exceptions. Remember, it is so much easier to hold on to a loyal customer than find a new one. Excellent customer service is the best form of advertising. Here in front of you either in person, by email or by phone or is someone who represents the reason your business exists. Look after your customers and make it a priority of your business to ensure that they are satisfied.

Summary of this chapter:

• Interruptions will happen. Aim to organise yourself so that they can be taken on board and noted for attention without deflecting you from the work at hand.

• If colleagues interrupt frequently, ask yourself, "why?". You must take steps to give them the direction and training they require to allow them get on with the job without needing to interrupt you unnecessarily. Make yourself available at set times to deal with necessary queries from colleagues.

• Customers are the reason you are sitting where you are. Forget this at your peril. If a customer interrupts, it is a call that needs attention. Organise yourself to provide excellent customer care.

Chapter 19 - Maintaining momentum

Have you ever spent hours on a project to the point where any get up and go which you may have had has left you? You are physically present, but you are not working at anything approaching your true ability. That is what happens if you plod along at the same work for an extended period.

Try to regain momentum by changing the topic, changing posture or direction at regular intervals. Please stand up, stretch, have a soft drink, take in some fresh air, but please do it make sure to wake yourself up.

Experience will show you your limit of concentration. Once you have discovered your limit, you must take care not to work uninterruptedly beyond that limit. If you plod along the result will be disappointingly out of proportion to the extra time spent.

Your posture is important. A change of posture can be as good as a change of work. If you have been sitting for half an hour on one project and yet feel the need to continue, why not take a five-minute break? Have a stretch, a brisk walk around, perhaps work on your feet for a while. Move to a standing desk. Change your work on hands at regular intervals which are related to your optimum concentration periods. Move on to something completely different and gain a second wind.

If one aspect of the project is heavily intellectual, why not move for a break to an area of the task that requires some physical effort or simply some creative thought?

If you move from one aspect of the job to another, try to ensure that you take a break at a natural cut off point. Before you stop, remember to decide and list your following matters for attention. End each aspect of the task on a planning note to make it easier to return later. Leaving a project high and dry in the manner of a crew suddenly abandoning the ship is counter-productive. You will waste time as you struggle to recall your last position when you return to the job. This loss is the opposite of what you are setting out to achieve through taking a break.

This change of task or change of physical position will have a recharging effect upon you. But remember that it may sometimes be essential for you to shut yourself off from the entire project at reasonably frequent intervals to recharge your batteries. Your work can gain from a necessary change of scene and a total break from the task.

Take note of your feelings as you progress through the day. Listen to your body. Watch out for signals that indicate "it is time for a change of scene", or "time for a break from this". Experiment with different approaches to your work. Find the one that suits you best just for now. Remember that you have not set your schedule in stone. You need not retain today's schedule forever. Put some changes into effect on an experimental basis and see how you get on. Be open to the possibility of adjusting your methods according to the nature of the work at hand.

Some jobs lend themselves to more extended periods of concentrated effort. In some instances, a pause can upset the momentum of activity. The break would be the opposite of what we wish to achieve in this chapter. But if you feel a slowing down of your mental energy or your physical ability, it could be a sign that you are plodding on when you should be changing the scene or taking a short break as a means of gaining renewed energy.

In all this is the idea is to keep your mind and body active. Your aim is to operate at a high level of efficiency. You have to avoid slipping into a somnolent state, something which can happen when you are intellectually overstretched by working on a complex task for an extended period. Add momentum to your work by trying out these techniques this week.

Summary of this chapter:

•   Don't plod on beyond your limit of optimum efficiency and effectiveness.

•   Change your body posture, change the angle of attack, take a break. But if you are taking a break, remember to pause at a logical point and, before the break, summarise your position, note the following steps and make it easy to return to the point where you left off.

•   Listen to your body responses. Know your limits and change your posture or the angle of work at the most appropriate intervals.

Chapter 20 - Action Sorter

Hopefully, you have seen the usefulness of a simple to-do list. It would help if you now gained the additional benefit of an action sorter sheet. The four action sorter squares you see here are where you will slot incoming items according to their relative importance and urgency.

The squares to the left refer to urgency. These are matters which are calling for attention now, but not all of them are important. You need to distinguish between the two and ensure that you attend to urgent and essential matters first. Examples would be medical or insurance emergencies, real crises and real deadlines for things that matter. These belong in the top left square. Other items may appear urgent, but you know that they are not so important in real terms. They are of little value. They may not even be your responsibility. They may have come to you in the form of interruptions. They may appear urgent, but they are less critical, and they are therefore entitled to less attention. Please place them in the bottom left square.

The squares to the right refer to items that are not urgent, but as you will see, some are important and some very important. Here you will have the likes of long-term health, fitness, training, crisis prevention, and planning all appropriate in the top right. These are important, but none are calling out for attention today. If you leave them to themselves, the danger is that they can be neglected and postponed. You must fit time into your schedule to attend to these important but less urgent items.

You will find time wasters and mindless autopilot activities in the bottom right square. They are neither urgent nor essential and have no place if you intend to devote your time efficiently to a project.

	MORE URGENT	LESS URGENT
MORE IMPORTANT		
LESS IMPORTANT		

Habitually making use of these classifications will revolutionise your approach to work. Make a habit of filling in a chart such as this last thing each evening to clarify the following day's priorities in your mind before finishing for the day. Then you can begin with confidence first thing the next day, happy in the knowledge that whatever interruptions occur, you have started the day by attending to your number one priority. Beware of the neglect of matters which appear in the top right square. Make sure to allocate time for these important but less urgent matters regularly so that you will not leave them on the back burner indefinitely.

Summary of this chapter:

•   Classify items according to urgency and importance.

•   Note the difference between urgency and importance.

•   Before you finish work for the day, set your priorities for the following day so the first thing you do when you return will be the most important and most urgent matter.

Part 4 — Recovery

"In this game, everyone needs a break to refuel, recharge, and jump back in full throttle."

— Helen Edwards,

Chapter 21 - Sometimes you need to run away

This book is about getting things done, managing time, clearing clutter, introducing certainty into your life and your plans. At times, simply keeping your work moving along can resemble a juggling act in a circus. And just as in a juggling act there can be slips, there are times in your working life when your whole system is in danger of collapse. This is a challenge for your ingenuity and your resilience, and it is what we will discuss in this chapter. You could call it "planned crisis running".

There will be times, hopefully not very often, when all hell breaks loose, and you are faced with what in power station terms would be termed an overload. You have come up against a combination of circumstances that are changing by the minute to the point where it is impossible to reduce the pressure by coming to a clear decision on action. The competing calls are such that you feel you cannot think clearly enough or logically enough to either delegate part of the crisis or put out the fires yourself.

Sometimes these crises are of your own making, arising from a failure to sufficiently plan ahead, procrastination, indecision, failure to delegate in time, a willingness to be distracted by lower priority interruptions, refusing to say "no" to unproductive projects and a general failure to prioritise your work. These factors drifting into one another over several projects and over time can and do lead to situations where a number of crises can hit simultaneously. Now they all clamour for your attention so pressingly that you can be frozen with indecision and even very real fear.

Such a combination of crises can be managed by a deliberate short period of running away. This is not running away from your responsibilities but a short period of black-out to enable you to think clearly again.

Clarity of thought is essential at such times and this cannot be achieved if you are on the receiving end of texts, emails, phone calls and a queue of unexpected callers all pressing for answers. Our communications, wonderful and indispensable as they are, can at times prevent adequate consideration of the matter in hand, with texts, phone calls and emails piling up before you have a chance to rationally respond to a difficult and fast-changing situation.

Faced with such a happening it is helpful to escape from the centre of it all for a short while. Get out of your office, away from the interruptions, leave the mobile behind you, get to a quiet anonymous place, a park, even a parking lot and stop for a while to relax, come into the moment, allow yourself to calmly consider the position and regain your equilibrium. Quieten yourself, bring down your pulse rate and relax. Remind yourself that you can overcome this problem. All you need is time, and you are making that necessary time now.

Have your notes with you so that when you have re-grouped your mental forces you can decide an order of priority in relation to the combination crises at hand. Some issue facing you must be of greatest importance. Release the pressure by deciding on a definite series of actions to deal with that issue, delegating subdivisions of the task wherever possible.

Other matters may require attention, crises also perhaps, but some must be of lesser importance than the first. Make a decision on each one in order of priority, deciding what should be done, by whom and when. See if there is a possibility of easing more of the build-up of pressure by gaining extensions of time on some of projects on a once off basis. But having gained breathing time resolve not to procrastinate further.

This chapter contains a formula for survival, not a normal method of work. If you work consistently to put the ideas of this book into practice you will seldom need to refer to this chapter. And rightly so. Firefighting and crisis management, unless your job, is not an efficient way of dealing with your work. And keep in mind your heart.

Summary of this chapter:

- Escape from an overwhelming crisis for a short while to enable you to regain your equilibrium and to logically decide how to deal with the problem on hand.

- Work out a strategy for dealing first with your main crisis, subdividing the problem and delegating as necessary. Do the same with any other current problems which may be troubling you, all in order of their importance.

- Avoid a recurrence by planning ahead and organising yourself better in the future.

Chapter 22 – Downtime - Sleep and Rest

It might appear odd in a book entitled "The Time of Your Life" to see a chapter devoted to sleep and taking it easy. You may have expected that every chapter would be advising you how you can get more and more done in less and less time. Apologies, but not in this chapter. Even the greatest workaholic will tell you that there is a point beyond which further work is counter-productive.

Remember that work is not the be-all and the end-all of your life. The work you do for a living is a means to an end. If you are lucky, you may be doing something that you find all-absorbing, an activity which you can enjoy as well. Build your schedule in such a way that there is plenty of opportunity for sleep, rest and play. Determine your optimum number of hours of sleep. Some people thrive on more, some on less. Without becoming paranoid about the subject, I advise you not to neglect it. If you burn a candle at both ends, you will spill wax and get burnt.

Shakespeare must indeed have given us the world's best definition of the benefits of sleep when, in Macbeth, he described it as that which "knits up the ravelled sleeve of care, sore labours bath, balm of hurt minds, great nature's second course, chief nourisher in life's feast".

Yet some look upon sleep and rest as a necessary evil, something like an unavoidable break from better things. They rise early and retire late, and in between, they fill their days with concerns way beyond the capacity of the day. We need to step off this treadmill of activity. We need to learn to take pleasure in doing nothing, in just watching the world go round.

Such is our tendency to organise ourselves that we sometimes introduce into our recreation more of the same pressures and deadlines that relaxation is supposed to relieve. In golf, we want to improve our score. Runners want to run faster and longer and, of course, keep ahead of the runner next to them. We set targets for fitness or excellence, even in what should be relaxed downtime. Remember that simultaneously burning two different coloured candles is almost as awkward and dangerous as burning one candle at both ends.

Learn to enjoy the game of golf just for the sake of company and enjoyment. Enjoy running just for relaxation, for improved fitness and for the fresh air. If you set a target, fix it in fun. Let recreation mean peace, unpressured and easy-going and the direct opposite to the everyday deadlines and targets that have become such a part of urban and even rural life in the 21st century.

Find time for family, children and friends and time for your thoughts. Pay attention to children and imitate them in their finding time to trust, to play and to explore. Children are amazed and enthused by the world around them. Follow their example. They look at the world and its people in a relaxed way, with a sense of wonder. Don't let that spirit die with time. Turn your free time into a period of genuine relaxation.

And if there still lurks in the back of your mind the idea that you are not doing enough, somewhere the idea that it is wrong not to be working, work to dampen any such thoughts and remind yourself that everything is okay. Let the world turn without you tonight. There are many things which are beyond our control so leave them where they are. It will help to recall and take to heart the serenity prayer "Lord grant me the serenity to accept the things I cannot change, the courage to change the things I can, and the wisdom to know the difference".

If history is anything by which to judge events, the Sun will rise tomorrow, and there will be more time for getting on with the work. Now it is evening and time for you to rest from your labours.

Summary of this chapter:

• Build time for rest and play into your schedule. Don't burn the candle at both ends.

• Don't introduce targets and deadlines into recreation. Enjoy it. Full stop.

• Remember to look at the world with childlike enthusiasm. Don't go to bed doubting if a new day will dawn tomorrow. The Sun came up yesterday. Without a doubt, it will rise again tomorrow. So take it easy tonight.

Chapter 23 - Exercise your body - Relax your mind

Some will read this heading and bemoan the short number of hours in the day. Far from relaxing, they wrongly claim that they need to work longer hours. But the key to productivity is the ability to get through the work effectively. For that, we need to step back regularly and relax and let the world turn without us.

Have you ever had a day when you decided to skip lunch and stick at your desk to clear a mountain of work? Did you ever take work home at night, logged in at night, during the weekend or even during the holidays to try to clear a backlog? If you have succumbed to this temptation, you will likely have found that your productivity afterwards has gone down. The late-night work has left you tired, irritable and indecisive the next day. The weekend of work has left you drained during the following week, and as for the part of the "holiday" spent working, well, we will not even contemplate the consequences of such a decision. The lesson has to be apparent; the longer the unbroken hours of work, the more the effectivity graph declines until you reach a point where you lose productive time. The solution is shorter, not more extended hours, not undivided attention but planned breaks from too long-drawn-out tasks.

You might protest that your work's importance and urgency is such that you do not have time to take a break. But the opposite is the case. This vital work is the reason you must take a break. Do this for the sake of the work itself, even if it were not true that there is more to life than work.

How can this be done, and where can you fit in relaxation? Look at it this way: if a vital client or customer asked you to allocate one hour for a daily meeting explaining that the required daily get together was an essential condition of his contract with you. If the client said that the period had to be guaranteed and uninterrupted, I imagine you would give serious thought to the request. In the case of a valuable client, you would almost certainly agree to the arrangement if you possibly could. So why not consider your exercise and relaxation break an appointment with an essential client, yourself, and set the time aside accordingly?

What form should the exercise take? That is a matter entirely for yourself. But it should be something that you can fit in regularly and without complications. It must be enjoyable; above all, it must not become another job you have to do. Some people enjoy solitude; for them, the idea of working out in the gym will be a nonstarter. Other people prefer the camaraderie that they find as part of working out with others.

When it comes to considering what type of exercise or relaxation break might suit you, there are some things to remember. You need to find something to fit into your day efficiently and without disruption. If your exercise planning involves travelling a distance to a running track, a pool or gym, then you may lapse at the first encounter with difficulty. Some people can set forth on a fitness plan and be entirely committed to carrying out such an undertaking. For them, there is no problem in switching off. Remember that very easiest of possibilities, walking, simply taking a walk at lunchtime. Walking does not usually require a change of clothing, and you can always appear as though you are going someplace even if you are not setting out to go anywhere in particular.

Remember, your mind requires relaxation just as much as your body needs exercise. You will have heard frequent urgings about the importance of physical activity for people working in sedentary occupations. Whatever you decide to do, please remember to take it easy at first. People who have not exercised for a time should take care, even to the point of seeking medical guidance before setting out on any new strenuous activity.

Remember these are instructions to improve your life quality. Hopefully, they might even extend it, but you do not want your life to come to a premature end. So please take it easy at first.

Summary of this chapter:

•   Remember the law of diminishing returns. Do not work day and night.

•   Make a regular appointment with yourself for relaxation and exercise.

•   Choose an activity that fits in comfortably with your lifestyle. Seek medical advice if you have not exercised recently.

Chapter 24 – Holidays

This chapter offers support to the spouses and partners of the true workaholic. It is the time of year that all (except workaholics) look forward to for months. Yes, it is time for holidays, a little free time for a change. It is time for a week or two way from the job. Lucky ones might escape for a month or more. For others, it might just be a well-deserved long weekend away from the usual routine of work.

When the day comes, leave the concerns of the office or business behind you. It is important, if you need to do so, to delegate the task of attending to your work while you are away. Avoid the regrettable tendency of some people in charge to continue to check back daily to satisfy themselves that everything - and everyone - is still under firm control.

Realise that you have worked hard for this. You need and deserve this break. Now get out there and enjoy it and leave the world to take care of itself for the duration. If you are still in doubt, ask yourself, "what would the people at work do if I died?" I hardly need to remind you that useful as we all are, after some little disruption (and hopefully a little sadness), the people back home would manage reasonably well without any of us. The world always moves on.

Some people depart on "vacation "with a library of professional literature and business books downloaded to catch up on their professional reading while on holidays. This is a pathetic approach to a holiday. Matters are bad enough because of the ready availability of mobile phones, texts, emails, tablets, and laptops. And naturally, the nagging fears that we are neglecting matters are not helped by the all singing all dancing high tech communication suites that mask as bedrooms in some top-class hotels.

True, it is difficult to escape from the web of communications that tends to bind us umbilically to our work, but flee from it we must. What we are in is indeed a trap. And you know what happens to an insect that gets caught in a web. The outcome is predictable and never positive.

Now there may be a need for communications from your work base in the case of extreme emergency or if some matter of critical importance arises. It might even be necessary to cut short the holiday to deal with the crisis in an extreme situation. You should meet this intervention by a determination to resume the holiday at the earliest opportunity. But the idea that an annual break would be interrupted by routine matters that are capable of being looked after back at base is simply beyond fitting words of rebuke. You deserve it, so please take and enjoy your holiday.

Some people find it genuinely difficult to get away for extended holidays. This situation is regrettable but understandable - in very particular circumstances. If this situation applies to you, why not take advantage of frequent short breaks and long weekends? Such short breaks cause little interference with day-to-day work. They can prove very useful, enjoyable and, most important, stress-free. They are brief enough to be unaffected by the pressures that can arise when we are arranging longer holidays.

Look upon the time away from work, holidays, as a particular source of recreation. Holidays provide an opportunity to recharge your physical and mental batteries and to rebuild energy and enthusiasm that can be put to practical use when you return to your work. So even the most ardent workaholic should see the advantage of holidays.

Chose a break that is truly different from your everyday routine. People whose work lives are passive will benefit from a more active holiday, subject to the usual medical precautions. On the other hand, people whose days are full of physical activity may gain the most benefit from the abandonment of almost anything associated with physical effort. It is pretty simple, suit yourself, but above all remember not to bring your work with you when you go on "holidays".

Summary of this chapter:

- Avoid workaholism. Take a holiday. In a rare situation where a crisis interrupts, take a replacement holiday at the earliest opportunity.

- Don't turn your hotel room into a remote control centre for your business's operation. Take a break; you know H O L I D A Y, cessation from work, recreation, a period of vacation. Cease from work – remember?

- If organising a long vacation causes you to stress, why not settle for several short breaks? If you believe that you are indispensable, ask yourself, "How did the world manage before I was born? "And consider (morbid thought I know) in the end it will have to survive without even you. So give your team a practice run in preparation for the tragedy to come! Enjoy a holiday.

Chapter 25 – Optimism wins

All kinds of people surround us. Some of these people are positive, some negative, and there are many shades of character in between. We interact with people all the time, and just as they pick up our moods, we pick up their vibes for good or ill.

We should try as far as possible to strike a positive note and avoid the moaning and the moaners. Our thoughts are intimately associated with our wellbeing. By repetition, the ideas that are going round in our minds affect our ability to remain positive. For this reason, we should try to think positive thoughts and associate with positive people.

We have all come across the moaner, the person who always sees the glass as half empty. In Ireland, our weather is quite changeable, and comment on the nature of the day is part and parcel of a friendly greeting. But the bright comment "Nice day, isn't it?" can be met by the moaner's response, "Yes, but will it last?" Some people insist on seeing a dark cloud obscuring every silver lining. It may not be the charitable thing to avoid a moaner, but if you are having one for company, it is necessary for your survival that you attempt to drown the moaner in a sea of optimism. Make it a policy to never accept a negative comment from anyone without offering something positive by way of a response.

Then there is the grumbler. I am sure you have come across someone who fits into this category. The grumbler is the one who constantly complains about something or other, including the performance of other people. An antidote to our tendency to grumble and find fault - and it can be very enlightening to try it - insists that for every complaint or grumble, you must mention three positive things about the moaned-about subject or person. This response is not just a counsel of charity, but necessity also. We all have several facets, and it is unhelpful if our dull side always appears without reference to the side that brightly shines.

Then there is the defeatist who will remind you of the pointlessness of the project. "This is someone else's work", "We have done this before", "There is no point in it anyway". How can enthusiasm flower in the arid garden of the defeatist? Not easy, but remember the cactus plant and recall that there are few places on Earth barren and lifeless. Getting enthusiasm to flower may prove difficult, but you can do it.

It will damage your effort to organise your time and your life if you succumb to the inertia of the moaner, the grumbler or the defeatist. "We can't do it" is a paralysing thought representing an almost absolute barrier to the effort. If you begin to doubt the value of a particular activity, it will not be easy to persuade yourself to invest the energy needed to bring the task forward. Simply put, doubt paralyses action.

If you aim to succeed, you must take care to fight off the doubter and the pessimist. If necessary, you must avoid the company of both. You must ensure that most of your activities and conversations are positive. You can most readily achieve this in the company of positive thinkers. Please eliminate the thought "impossible" from your vocabulary and your mind. There is nothing more calculated to leave you in the doldrums then the belief that something is impossible. Remember that most things are responsive to diligence and effort.

Seek out positive people with whom to exchange your plans and hopes. Inspire positive thoughts and beware of people with a predisposition towards pessimism. If you are asked, "How are you?" don't treat it as an invitation to speak at length about your problems and worries. Reserve the detailed answer for an occasional heart to heart with someone, an optimist, whom you know well enough. Allow yourselves an annual mutual moan if it is essential for either of you.

You should liberally sprinkle your actions and plans with this sort of optimism. Use positive language, letting through idealism, hope for the future and a non-wavering belief that what you seek can be achieved through the dedicated pursuit of your plans.

Summary of this chapter:

- Avoid moaners, avoid moaning and don't join in when other people moan.

- Introduce optimism into your thoughts and your phrases.

- Associate with optimistic people, people who believe that everything is possible for those who apply themselves with diligence and effort.

Part 5 – Time Saving Tips

"Time flies fast, but it's good you are the pilot. Just control your time well away from hijackers. Save time profitably; Spend time productively!"

— Israelmore Ayivor

Chapter 26 – Staying in the Present Moment

We can tend to lament the past and daydream about the future. Neither of these approaches is very useful. We must come to realise that this present moment is the only time that is ours to use.

We need to accept that for better or worse, the past is the past. Certain decisions, actions, failures to decide, failures to act, we have taken or not taken these actions in earlier moments of our lives, and these have brought us to where we are right now. It might be interesting to speculate about what changes we would make if only we could live life again. But it is pointless to daydream about something that can never be. However, there is one change which we would all wish. If we had a chance to start over, I believe our wish would be to decide to live in the present moment.

Some people live a significant part of their lives in the future. They spend their time thinking of what might be in this or that situation. For some, the consideration of the future can be a nightmare lived in the present, as they contemplate the worst of all possible scenarios. Yet tomorrow is precisely that, a day in the future. And while we should provide for it and plan for it, our provisions and plans must be centred on what we can do right now to help make tomorrow as we would wish tomorrow to be.

The key to real achievement rests in making effective use of the present moment. All that we see around us, every one of the scientific discoveries, the medical breakthroughs, the architectural and technological wonders, result from human activity in some time, which was then the present moment. Of course, there was planning, but above all else, there was action. That action has produced the results which we enjoy and observe all around us. Everything that we have today is the product of someone's activity in the past. Similarly, by engrossing ourselves now in worthwhile activities, we can build a better world for ourselves, our children and our grandchildren.

There are many things that we plan to do sometime. When the time is right, we will go on that memorable holiday. When we get a chance, we will spend more time with the kids; we will study philosophy and figure out the world's nature. We will make a fortune, invent the indispensable object, write that book. We will compose that song, clear the garage, start a new business, become president of the corporation (or the country). We will propose marriage, create a family, design a fantastic app or an indispensable program. We will study a language, learn about management or computers, move to a new house or plant a tree. Some day when things are just right, we will do everything we have ever dreamt of doing, everything we have put on the long finger. Someday, we will fly to the moon or Mars, but only when the circumstances are just right.

When will we realise that this is the moment of decision, this is the opportune time, this is the time for action, for activity, for progress, for renewal? This moment is the appropriate time.

I hope this book will bring you many hours of practical reflection. I hope you will take it up and look through it time and time again, finding today a chapter that answers your needs of today, and tomorrow something that is inspiring for tomorrow. I do not intend that you read this book from cover to cover in one or even several sessions. You will find the chapters grouped in associated parts, but they are not listed in order of importance. The idea is that you can open any one chapter even now and obtain some benefit today without reference to any other chapter.

If you can manage to take one chapter today and apply its suggestions for this week, and if you follow the same procedure again next week and the week after, I hope you may, in a short time, succeed in upgrading all your activities and so gain for yourself that most precious of all commodities, the Time of Your Life.

Summary of this chapter:

- The past is water under the bridge; the future is yet to be. In between is this present moment. Now is the time available for you to use.

- Everything that we have now is the result of some action taken at some time, which was then a present moment.

- Yes, dream but don't live in your dreams. Take some action now to help your dreams come to pass. Work today to help make your dreams come true.

Chapter 27 - Speed Reading

There are techniques which you can learn and which you can use to increase dramatically the amount which you can read, and take in, in a given time. Speed reading is a way of more efficiently taking in helpful information in your life and work.

To be avoided is the habit of reading material on a word-by-word basis. Try instead to absorb ideas and sentences as units. Avoid sub vocalisation as you read, the tendency to silently form words in your mind as you go along. This practice slows down your speed of reading to the rate at which you can speak. This rate is much slower than the speed at which you can comprehend.

At the next opportunity, practice the art of taking in the idea of a sentence without forming the individual words in your mind. Why not practice this technique when next reading a newspaper or an article?

There are other valuable tips for taking in the content of written material:

Scanning

Scan the index of a book before setting off to read through the book page by page. Often a book will have a detailed introduction or a chapter summary. These notes will give an outline of what you will find in each chapter. A quick review of these summaries will provide you with an overview of the book—this could avoid you having to read entire book.

Quick and often

Years ago, as a student, I was given a tip that has proved invaluable to me in absorbing written material. The rule was "read it quickly but often". In that way, you obtain an overview, and, after several readings, the entire content can fall into place and in context. A beneficial effect of the "quick but often" technique is that after a few such flash readings, you will find it possible to recall or review the book's content almost as quickly as you can turn the pages.

Very technical matters will require a different reading approach compared with a method appropriate for lighter materials. They cannot be glossed over quickly with any reasonable expectation that the content will be understood and retained. But even in technical matters, a quick first glance will be an excellent introduction to the book overall and will prove helpful when you come to study the book in detail.

In your enthusiasm to improve your reading speed, remember it is important not to lose sight of the fundamental question, "do I need to read this at all?" You will save the most time if you can ignore the particular book or article completely. It may be possible to have someone else conduct a preliminary vetting of material for your consideration. By that means, you need only concern yourself (if at all) with pre-marked highlights of material that has passed that preliminary test.

If you receive a book or magazine and are only concerned with one or two articles, these can be scanned and filed for attention. You should avoid slipping into the time-wasting habit of automatically browsing through the entire of any magazine that happens to come before you.

Some magazines have a helpful feature. The help consists of a summary of each article at a certain point in each issue. These summaries provide an overview of each topic, and you can more easily decide if the entire article represents necessary reading or not.

Set yourself a time limit for the reading of any particular piece of material. Cut the time a little short to help you to develop the habit of moving along more quickly. Avoid backtracking to check on something that you have already read. Develop the confidence to move on. If you are reading quickly, you might move your finger down as you read and, in that way, force your mind to move along as promptly as your finger.

Summary of this chapter:

- Scan before you read to see if something is worth reading at all. Note any summaries and pick out for reading only what is of interest to you.

- Read without sub vocalisation. You can take in ideas more quickly than you can speak. So why talk to yourself silently as you read? Practice this when reading the newspapers.

- Read quickly and often. After several readings, you may find the whole book falling into memory and in context.

Chapter 28 - Time on the Move

It seems most of us spend about one-third of our lives asleep. But have you ever stopped to consider the percentage of your waking day you spend on the move? Are you commuting in the morning, and again in the evening? Are you perhaps travelling also in the course of the day?

The first question to ask yourself relates to commuting and travelling time. Is it necessary? Can this travelling be avoided? Can this waste of time be reduced?

Some ideas:

With so means of video conferencing available to us, there is less reason for any of us to travel from one place to another for routine meetings.

If you cannot find employment nearer to where you live and if you must be physically present, could you move more closely to the job? Have you balanced the value of your time lost in commuting against the cost of moving home? You may have taken transport into account in deciding on your present location, but what about the value of your own time? How much does it cost you when you lose an extra hour in traffic morning and evening every working day? What about the stress of rush hour traffic if you drive? And what about the stress of travelling by public transport if that is your means of getting to work?

What if your position is that neither you nor your work can move closer to the other? Might there be an option to work from home for even part of the time? In 2020 the Coronavirus Crisis reminded us of the practicality of working from home in our always-connected world. If you do have to travel, what about avoiding the heaviest traffic? Can you leave ahead of it or after the worst of it? Thanks to GPS and Google Maps, we can see the current state of traffic on our planned route and use predictions based on past traffic records to help us manage our travel times more efficiently. What about arranging your life so that you are driving against rush hour traffic? Think of the possibilities that flexitime now offers people in so many places of work. Above all, try to avoid beginning your day by sitting in a traffic jam. That beginning is the opposite of the motivation you require to get your working day off to a dynamic start.

Perhaps you have reduced travelling time to the point where you cannot effectively cut it any further. Well done, you have begun to free some of your time for better use. So how might you make use of the remaining time spent on the move? Despite the considerable number of radio stations available, you do not have to listen to what might happen to be on the radio at any particular time. Why not try an audiobook, learn a new language, listen to a podcast, learn how to improve a skill? Lifelong learning can take place on the move. And if you are learning something new and unfamiliar, you can help the process along by repeating the recordings as often as you wish, and always taking care as you drive.

But it is not all a matter of learning and developing new skills while on the move. Relax and take it easy by listening to your favourite music. We all know that music can change our mood. Use that fact to your advantage, particularly in the mornings, to help you get off to a great start. Use it in the evenings to help you relax at the end of a busy day.

The purpose of this advice is not to encourage you to fill every available minute with productive activity. There is more to life than productivity.

Remember to read and apply Chapter 23 – (Exercise and Rest). But as we can find commuting to be tedious and boring it is helpful to remember that there are possibilities available to us. These can be brought into play from time to time whenever we feel we need to make better use of your time spent on the move.

Summary of this chapter:

- Avoid losing time on the move. Work remotely where possible. Bring home and work nearer to each other if you can. Avoiding travel at busy times.

- Consider making use of time on the move. Learn a language, acquire a skill but don't forget the value of simple relaxation as well. But in all this, please, whatever you do, keep your mind on the road.

- Music can change your mood. Use music to assist you before the start and at the end of the working day.

Chapter 29 – Capturing ideas

Have you ever awoken having dreamt of what seemed like a brilliant idea? It might have been the inspiration for a book. It could be a beneficial thought or a call to action. It could be a simple reminder about a book you wish to read or a film you would like to see. It might be a prompt that you need to call a friend, or it could even be an idea for a life-changing invention. We have all had this experience. The thought appears at the time to be something that you could not possibly forget. The idea seemed so vivid that it would be hard to imagine you could lose it by the time you got out of bed. Yet here you are, hours later trying to recall just what was that great idea. This failure of memory is an all-too-common experience, and, in this chapter, I will offer you a method that you can use to capture all these floating ideas.

We waste much time repeating messages to ourselves, consciously trying not to forget something which flashed briefly across our minds. Yet, we can neglect to equip ourselves with the means to recall better what we wish to remember. It is necessary to develop the habit of recording these ideas and flashes of inspiration as soon as they come to you. If you capture the thought, you free yourself from the liability of having to take immediate action on the idea. The idea has been noted forward for action later, and it remains safely there until you have time to act upon it.

You can capture thoughts and ideas in any way that happens to be convenient at the time. It can be a simple note on a yellow sticky pad or written on a scrap of paper that might happen to be lying near to hand when the idea strikes. The most important thing is to get the idea down somewhere. But you can lose scraps of paper. And notes written on several sticky pads can quickly grow out of control. Therefore, a more secure method would be only to use these paper notes as very temporary storage. We are all discouraged from bringing our electronic devices to bed, so pencil and paper near our bedside make sense as a temporary storage area for ideas captured in the night.

The great news is that our electronic devices can store all these miscellaneous thoughts, ideas and inspirations until we have a chance to put them into effect. Apart from bedtime, we have our devices with us most of the time. There is no need for us to lose track of an idea or to allow ourselves to drown in a sea of disorganised notes and papers.

Make no mistake about it, and no matter where you are when you think of an idea, you will lose that flash of inspiration unless you capture it somehow. Take no chances. If you want to grab a thought, get it down somewhere, anywhere. In this way, you can capture every moment of illumination. And you will more usefully employ your time if you no longer have work to try to recall fleeting ideas that have been allowed to slip by without you having taken note at the time.

Our electronic devices allow us to bring all these thoughts and ideas together in one place, and that one place does not have to be on the one device in our pockets. Thanks to cloud computing, what we capture in one location can be accessed later wherever we may happen to be. We can take a photograph, a screengrab, a GPS location, note an address, a name, a phone number, anything we wish, and we can store it safely and securely in our notes for future reference.

These electronic memos can themselves drift out of control unless you organise these notes into folders and categories. You can store incoming messages temporarily in a general location or cover folder. But they need to be transferred after a little while into a named folder where they belong. But these notes must not become a secondary to-do list. They are coming in at random, and so they need to be looked at later and incorporated into your actual to-do list (see Chapter 13) so that you can attend to them at the appropriate time.

With the temporary aid of simple paper and pencil, supported by your everyday electronic devices, you never need again to lose sight of a bright idea or fail to remember something you need to do.

Summary of this chapter:

• Don't lose that idea. Jot it down even temporarily before it slips your mind.

• Remember to transfer temporary paper notes to your electronic note system before the paper notes fall into confusion.

• Keep your electronic notes organised in folders, like with like, so that they will be more easily found and transferred into your to-do list.

Chapter 30 – So you have gained time?

The purpose of this book is to offer you tips on time management and decision-making, helping you to take care of your precious time. I want you to save time at home and in your work and help you avoid the paralysis that comes from indecision.

Imagine the time that you would save if you applied even some of the ideas contained in this book. What you do with this time is a matter for yourself. You have hopefully gained the time, so you are entitled to spend it as you wish. Workaholism is to be discouraged. But if that is how you relate to life and if you want to spend the time you have saved at work by doing still more work, fair enough. Horses for courses, and after all, this is the Time of YOUR Life.

The more efficient use of the time of your life must improve your morale and your lifestyle. It must make available to you some free time you may wish to devote to your family and friends, time which you might use for community and leisure pursuits. Please try not to create a second job out of your leisure by introducing impossible deadlines and unreal targets. But at the end of the day, it is your time, is the time of your life.

These practices will free time that you might like to spend in reflection. You might at last find time for contemplation and meditation. You might become more recollected, have time for the serious questions, to better consider the question of who you are, speculate as to why are you here, and question what do you plan to do with your life. Take your voyage of self-discovery seriously but not too seriously. Make space for fun also.

You can take time to tend your garden and contemplate your navel if that is what you wish. You can take care of your waistline, and at the same time, you can engage in reading and musing about the very meaning of existence. It is all up to you. You cannot say now that you lack the time for all these exciting, fascinating and practical activities. In short, you can gain time to discover and rediscover; you can gain time to step off the treadmill. The treadmill seems such a part of life today, yet we don't often take the time to ask ourselves why we are on it.

All this should whet your appetite for saving a little of the precious time that seems to pass over us all so very quickly. Capture time today as it passes. Notice that time is like milk. And just like milk, you have to use it before its expiry date. Much of our time is wasted in regret about our yesterdays and worry about our tomorrows. Just consider how little of your time today has been spent consciously appreciating the fact that you are here right now and that this present moment is yours.

You can use the time you gain for anything of your own choice. The world and your community are crying out for volunteers to participate in community building and providing aid to people in need. But if you ask them to participate, many people will tell you, "I do not have the time". This book will helpfully remove that obstacle for some.

For a minute, consider the alternatives. Some of these other options don't bear thinking about. Think of getting yourself into time-losing situations, rising late, getting caught in traffic. Think of getting to work late, getting off to a bad start, losing time all day. Imagine leaving your job late, getting home late and exhausted, all the while wondering what you have achieved in an unplanned and distracted day, then falling into bed late and tired. Imagine the next day waking up too late and too tired to get off to a fresh start. Hopefully, this is not an image of most of us most of the time. But if you see that there is some resemblance to how things are with you, you need to select, read, and apply parts of this book.

We all have the same number of minutes in a day. Some use these minutes to organise the affairs of the world. Others cannot find the time to write a letter to a distant friend. It has to be of benefit if you can save time to devote to simple things like that.

Life is given to us a minute at a time. Use this book to make good use of it. Don't let the time of your life slip by unnoticed. Now is the Time of Your Life. Enjoy the journey.

Summary of this chapter:

- If you gain time by reading this book, then that time is yours to use as you wish.

- Consider the effect of living a life where time is being lost, and a life is being lived in a disorganised way. There has to be a better way than this for you to organise your life.

- We all share an equal number of hours in the day. Life comes to us a minute at a time. Put time to good use now. Don't let the Time of Your Life pass unnoticed. Enjoy.

About the Author

Tony Brady is based in Dublin Ireland

His earlier books include:

- Just for Today (also available as an audio book)
- The Gratitude Response
- A Wave of Blessing
- Simply Calling God

He contributes audio meditations to the Insight Timer Meditation App at www.insighttimer.com/tonybrady where his contributions have been listened to more than a million times

His meditations focus on themes such as as gratitude, positivity forgiveness, making use of the time of our lives and beginning again

He lives with his wife Fran, an environmental activist, in Dublin, Ireland.

See more at www.lifeofmindfulness.com

13637390R00063